OK

funky room decorating

SCHOLASTIC INC.

New York   Toronto   London   Auckland   Sydney
Mexico City   New Delhi   Hong Kong   Buenos Aires

door memo page 36

jewelry holder page 38

shaped cushions page 40

tissue box page 46

painted flowers page 50

lampshade page 54

storage boxes page 58

about this book

Hey, friends,

Welcome to the world of funky decorating! Ever dreamed of being an interior designer?

Get set to impress your friends and family with an awesome bedroom makeover—made by you! These fun and unique projects are designed to glitz up any room.

Let your creativity run wild, follow the easy instructions and, for extra fun if you're feeling clever, why not personalize your creations to suit you or your best friend! Transform your room from dull into daring! With these projects, your room will be looking glam in no time! And hey, if you're really skilled, Mom may even let you make an item or two to put elsewhere in the house—cool!

Make these fab creations by yourself or grab some friends and put your creativity to use while you chat! What could be more fun?

These hip decorator ideas can also make great presents for friends and family!

So what are you waiting for?

Are you ready to inject some funk into your bedroom?

Now let's get started.

1 Choose your favorite project.

2 Grab all the materials you will need.

3 Read through all the steps before you start.

4 Protect your work surface with plastic. It's not cool to mess up a good table!

5 Get some help if you get stuck.

6 Have lots of fun!

Look out for the star ratings on each project.

nice & easy!

step it up!

like a pro!

let's get started!

rainbow wall

like a
pro!

things you need

- white wall
- acrylic paints — pink, purple, yellow, green, red, blue, orange, black & white
- paintbrushes — assorted sizes
- pencil & paper
- clear acetate & permanent black marker (optional)
- overhead projector (optional)
- drop cloths

1 Before you can paint the wall, you will need to transfer the rainbow pattern onto the wall. There are three different ways you can do this:

- Using a grid
- Using an overhead projector
- Drawing freehand

2 Using a Grid
Draw the grid lines on your wall. Make sure they are parallel to the floor and side walls. If you draw 4-inch (10.2 cm) squares on your wall, the design will be 5 feet (1.5 m) high and 10 feet (3.1 m) long.

You can make the design smaller, or you can choose not to include everything in it — just the rainbow if you like!

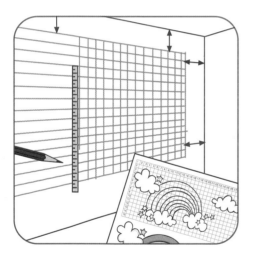

3 Using an Overhead Projector
Trace the pattern onto clear acetate using a permanent black marker. Position the overhead projector with the pattern in front of the wall and adjust until you have the image projected onto the wall exactly where you want it.

Now just draw the pattern on the wall with a pencil! Too easy!

4 If you have a really steady hand, you can try drawing the design onto your wall freehand with a pencil!

Warning — this is tricky!

5 Lay out the drop cloths. Make the rainbow colors lighter with white paint. Paint the rainbow and stars. Next paint the shading with the darker colors and the blue background and then the black outline last of all!

Now you have your very own awesome "sky" on your bedroom wall!

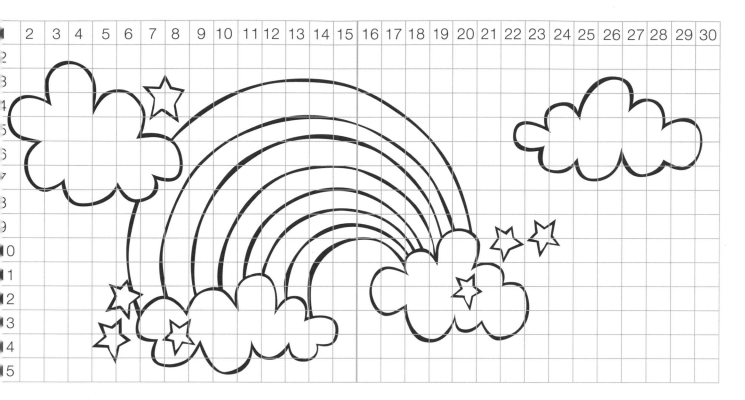

| | 2 | 3 | 4 | 5 | 6 | 7 | 8 | 9 | 10 | 11 | 12 | 13 | 14 | 15 | 16 | 17 | 18 | 19 | 20 | 21 | 22 | 23 | 24 | 25 | 26 | 27 | 28 | 29 | 30 |

9

desk set

step it
up!

things you need

- wooden pencil box
- wooden pencil holder
- diary
- white poster board
- felt — white, green, yellow & orange
- 1/8-inch (3 mm) foam sheeting
- 5 blue gems
- cotton fabric — orange & pink
- acrylic paints — orange & pink
- varnish
- paintbrush
- pencil
- paper
- ruler
- spray adhesive
- craft glue
- scissors
- craft knife

desk mat

1 Measure and cut out two rectangles of poster board 13 x 18 inches (33 x 45.7 cm) and two long strips measuring 13 x 2 inches (33 x 5 cm).

2 Lay each poster board piece on the orange fabric and cut out the fabric to fit, allowing an extra 1 1/2 inches (3.8 cm) around the edges.

3 Attach the fabric to each piece of poster board using the spray adhesive.

For the rectangles, first glue the corners, then the sides.

For the two strips, glue only the sides, leave the ends!

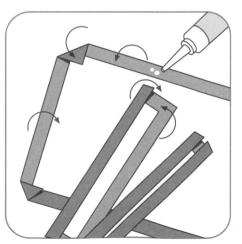

11

4 Position the two strips on the front of one of the rectangles, 1 inch (2.5 cm) in from each side.

Fold the end fabric flaps over onto the back and glue.

Next glue the two rectangles together—fabric sides showing!

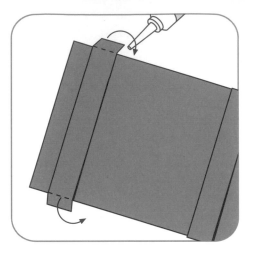

5 Transfer two large flowers (page 15) onto the poster board, one with a stem and one without. Cut them out carefully with a craft knife. Ask an adult to help! Use the same pattern to cut out felt pieces of the flowers and glue these onto the poster board flowers.

Glue a blue gemstone in the center of each flower.

6 Glue the flowers onto the strips on the desk mat. You now have a really cool mat that you can use to hold sheets of paper!

diary

7 Open your diary and lay it on top of the pink fabric. Cut out the fabric to fit, allowing 1 1/2 inches (3.8 cm) around all sides.

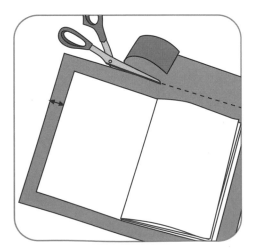

8 Attach the foam sheeting to the front cover of the diary using the spray adhesive and trim it back around the edges to fit the book.

9 Attach the fabric to the front and back covers of the diary using the spray adhesive. Lay the open diary on top of the fabric. Push it down so that the fabric really sticks.

Close the diary to check that it is not too tight!

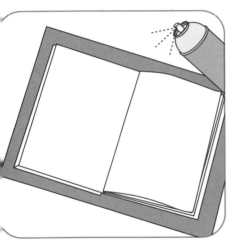

10 Open up the diary again. Fold over the edges of the fabric and glue it down, doing the corners first and then the sides. Cut a slit at the spine so the fabric can be folded.

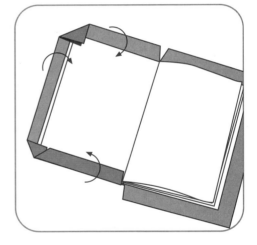

11 Glue the first and last pages to the inside covers to hide the fabric edges!

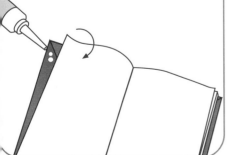

12 Cut out the felt pieces of a large flower with a stem from felt and glue them onto the front of the diary.

pencil boxes

13 Paint 1-inch (2.5-cm) wide pink and orange stripes on the outside of each box and paint the inside orange.

The boxes may need two coats of paint. Let dry and then varnish.

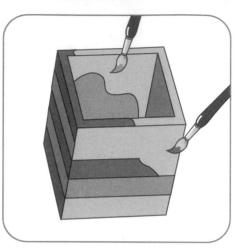

14 Cut out a small poster board flower with stem. Use the same pattern to cut out the felt pieces for the flower and glue them onto the poster board flower.

Glue a blue gemstone in the center. Glue the flower to the inside of the pencil holder.

15 Cut a piece of green felt to fit around the pencil and overlap slightly. Glue it on.

16 Cut out a small poster board flower. Use the same pattern to cut out the felt pieces for the flower and glue them on.

Glue a blue gemstone in the center. Glue the flower onto the end of the pencil.

flower patterns

painted
wastepaper
basket

⭐
⭐

step it
up!

16

things you need

- wooden wastepaper basket
- acrylic paints—pink, purple, yellow, green, red, blue, orange & white
- 4 wooden balls
- varnish
- purple feather boa
- paintbrush & pencil
- craft glue & wood glue
- scissors

1 Paint the inside and outside of the wooden wastepaper basket with the white paint. Let dry and then transfer the pattern on page 19 onto all four sides of the outside of the basket.

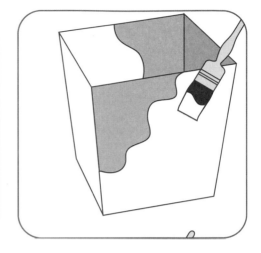

2 Paint the inside and outside of the wastepaper basket with the pink paint. It will probably need two coats.

3 Paint all the circles next. Use the white paint to lighten the colors. Use a darker mix of each color to paint a semi-circle at the base of each circle.

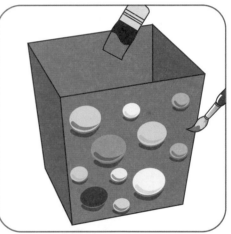

4 Paint the wooden balls in four different colors and, when dry, glue them onto the corners of the base of the wastepaper basket using the wood glue.

Let them dry well before the next step!

5 When the paint and glue are dry, apply two coats of varnish all over the wastepaper basket including the wooden balls.

Let dry overnight.

6 Glue the feather boa around the top of the wastepaper basket, overlapping ends slightly.

With your new ultracool wastepaper basket, now even your trash can be groovy!

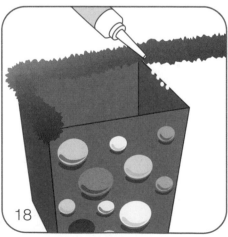

18

door curtain

things you need

- wood molding & saw
- 2 small screw-in rings & 2 cuphooks
- orange acrylic paint
- varnish
- paintbrush
- assorted ribbons
- assorted flowers (approx. 140)
- craft glue
- tape measure & scissors

1 Saw two pieces of molding measuring the width of your door. Ask an adult to help. Paint the rounded sides of the molding orange and then varnish. Let dry.

2 Measure from the top of the door frame to just above the floor—unless you're super-tall, you may need to grab an adult to help with this! Cut ten pieces of ribbon this length.

3 Glue one end of each ribbon onto one of the flat sides of one piece of molding. Start in 2 inches (5 cm) from each end and space the ribbons out evenly.

To keep the other end of each ribbon from fraying, fold up 1 inch (2.5 cm) and glue.

4 Glue the flat sides of the molding together and then screw in the rings 2 inches (5 cm) from each end.

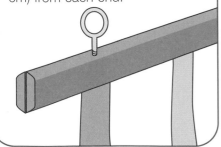

5 With the point of the scissors, make small holes along each ribbon, spacing them about every 6 inches (15 cm). Pull the sepal off the back of each flower, push stem through the hole and then replace the sepal. Keep going until you have decorated all the ribbons with flowers!

To hang, screw the cuphooks into the door frame in line with the rings.

21

things you need

- cotton fabric—red & pink
- poster board
- 1/4 inch (6 mm) foam sheeting (optional)
- pencil & paper
- craft glue
- spray adhesive
- craft knife
- scissors
- double-sided tape

1 Decide how big you want your name sign and then enlarge the pink heart (page 24) and letters (pages 26 & 27) that you need. The sign would look really cool above your bed or on your door!

Transfer the patterns onto the poster board and cut out with a craft knife. Ask an adult to help with this part!

2 Glue the right side of the poster board letters onto the wrong side of the red fabric, leaving space between each letter. Let dry.

3 Next cut out each letter, allowing 1 inch (2.5 cm) around the edges.

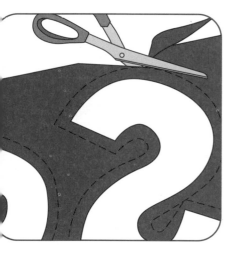

4 Fold the 1 inch of fabric in around the letters and glue it down. Sometimes you will need to notch the fabric to fold it over and glue down.

5 If there are holes in the letters, like in an "O," then you need to punch a hole in the fabric and cut the curves so that you can fold the fabric over and glue.

6 If you want to pad your heart, attach it onto the foam sheeting using spray adhesive. Let dry and then trim around the edge.

7 Attach the foam side of the heart if you have padded it or just the poster board if you haven't, onto the pink fabric using the spray adhesive.

Cut out the fabric allowing 1 1/2 inches (3.8 cm) around the edge.

8 Fold the fabric down around the heart. Sometimes you will need to notch the fabric to fold it over and glue down.

Check it out!
We're getting there!

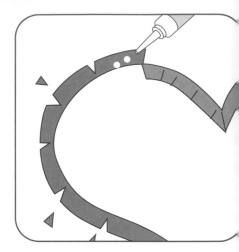

9 Glue on the letters.

10 Attach your heart name sign to the wall or door with double-sided tape.

heart patterns

25

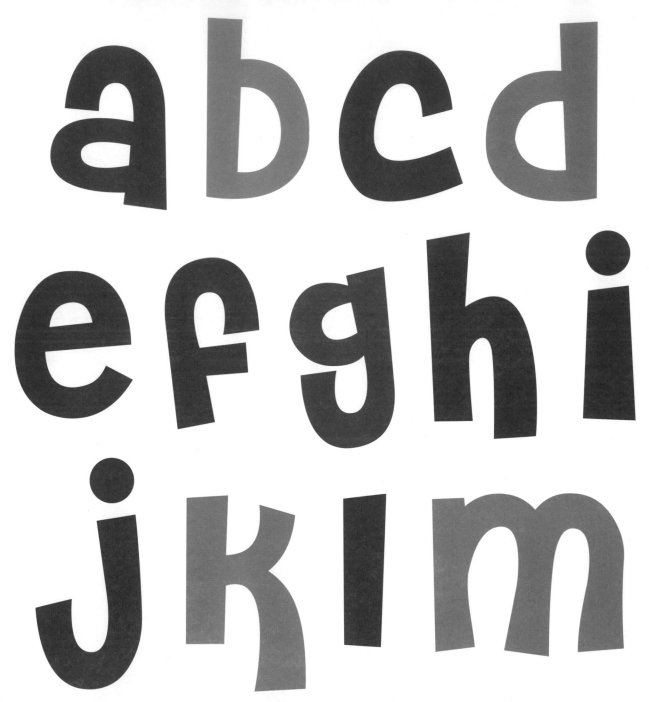

things you need

- cork bulletin board
- acrylic paints — purple, white, yellow, green & blue
- white poster board
- push pins
- paintbrushes — small & medium
- craft knife
- ruler
- pencil

1 Paint the cork side of the bulletin board with the white paint. Let dry and then, using a pencil and ruler, draw in the lines for the striped pattern.

Make the stripes different widths, for a funky look!

2 Paint each stripe a different color. Mix the colors with the white paint if you need to lighten them.

Looking groovy already!

3 Transfer the flower pattern (page 30) onto the white poster board and make as many flowers as you like.

Cut each one out with the craft knife—ask an adult to help!

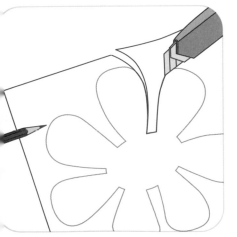

4 Paint the flowers to match the striped pattern and, when they are dry, pin them on the board for a cool look!

flower pattern

31

like a
pro!

lips throw rug

32

things you need

- red fake fur fabric
- polyester padding
- red fleece fabric
- red sewing thread
- black permanent marker
- scissors
- pins
- sewing machine

1 Decide how big you would like your lips throw rug. Is it going to go on your bed or look really fab on the floor?

Then purchase enough fake fur fabric, fleece, and padding, including at least 2 inches (5 cm) as a seam allowance.

2 Transfer the lips pattern (page 35) onto the wrong side of the fake fur using a black permanent marker.

Make sure you include the lip line through the center.

3 Stitch along the lip line in the center before continuing.

4 Cut around the outside edge of the fur lips, leaving a seam allowance of 1 inch (2.5 cm).

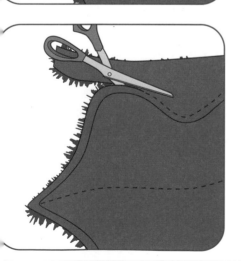

5 Pin the three layers together.

Start with the padding on the bottom, then the fleece (fluffy side up), and place the fake fur (fur side down) on top.

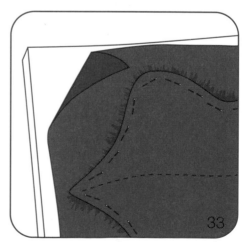

6 Sew around the lip edge of all the layers, leaving a 1-inch (2.5 cm) seam allowance.

Leave an 8-inch (20.3 cm) opening on one of the flat edges for turning the lips to the right side.

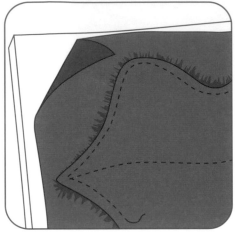

7 Trim the fleece and padding to match the edge of the fur lips.

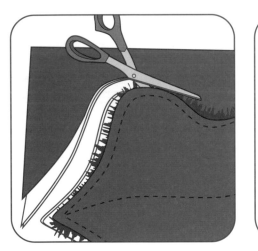

8 Turn the lips to the right side and neatly hand-stitch the opening closed for a hot set of lips!

Step onto this!

lips pattern

nice & easy!

door memo

back in '10'
see ya then!

36

things you need

- wooden door hanger
- light blue acrylic paint
- medium paintbrush
- oven-bake modeling clay—green, orange, pink, purple, blue & yellow
- baking pan, foil & kitchen knife
- clear glitter paint
- craft glue
- small note pad & pencil

1 Roll out the purple modeling clay until it is 1/2 inch (13 mm) thick and make a base piece the same size as the rainbow below.

Make a groove through the middle using the pencil. This groove needs to be big enough to slide the pencil through when the rainbow is glued on top.

2 Shape the green, orange, pink and yellow modeling clay into ropes that are 1/2 inch (13 mm) thick. Make a rainbow the same size as the pattern.

3 Make two purple stars and one blue star. Bake all the pieces in the oven following the instructions on the package. Ask an adult for help.

4 Paint the wooden door hanger on both sides with the blue paint and let dry. Glue on the purple base piece, the rainbow on top, and then the stars. Paint with clear glitter paint and let dry. Glue on the small note pad and slide in the pencil.

Write cool messages to your family and friends! Wild!

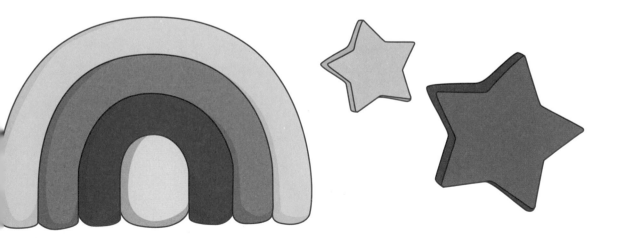

jewelry holder

like a
pro!

things you need

- cotton fabric — red, pink & orange
- poster board
- 1/4-inch (6-mm) foam sheeting
- 14 inches (35.5 cm) narrow ribbon
- pencil & paper
- craft glue & spray adhesive
- craft knife
- scissors
- large decorative pins

1 Decide on how big you want your jewelry holder and then enlarge the heart patterns on page 24. Transfer the patterns to poster board and cut out the hearts with a craft knife.

You will need two large hearts, one medium and one small. Ask an adult to help with this part!

2 Glue one of the large hearts onto the red fabric. Cut out the fabric around the heart, allowing 2 inches (5 cm) around the edges.

Attach foam sheeting to one side of each of the other hearts using the spray adhesive. Let dry and then trim the foam around the edges of the poster board.

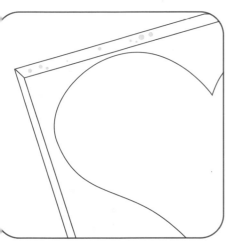

3 Attach the foam side of the large heart to the red fabric using the spray adhesive. Attach the foam side of the medium heart to the pink fabric, and attach the foam side of the small heart to the orange fabric.

Cut out the fabric around each heart, allowing 2 inches (5 cm) around the edges.

4 Fold and glue down the fabric around each heart. Sometimes you will need to notch the fabric to fold it over and glue down.

Looking cool, huh?

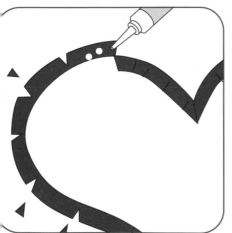

5 Pierce two holes in the large unpadded red heart, thread the narrow ribbon through to the back, and knot to make a hanger. Glue the large red hearts together and then, on the padded side, glue on the pink heart and then the orange heart.

Use the large pins to attach your fab collection of jewelry and accessories.

like a
pro!

things you need

- cotton fabric — white, dark pink, pink & orange
- fabric paints — yellow, white, green, pink, blue, black, dark pink & purple
- paintbrushes — small & medium
- plastic
- masking tape
- iron
- clean cloths
- polyester filling
- needle & matching threads
- pencil & paper
- scissors
- pins
- sewing machine

1 Enlarge the cushion patterns (pages 43, 44 & 45) to the size you would like your cushions to be.

Transfer the patterns onto the white fabric with a pencil.

Cut out each cushion design, allowing 2 inches (5 cm) around the edges.

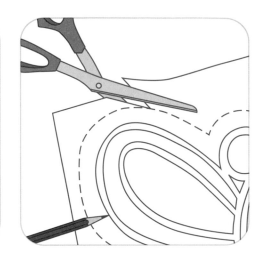

2 Cover your work surface with plastic, lay the cushion designs on top and keep them in place with masking tape.

3 Paint on the designs, using the patterns as a guide. If you need to, lighten the colors with white paint. Paint the black outline last.

4 Let the designs dry overnight.

Then, using a clean cloth on top and underneath each cushion design, iron on medium heat for a few minutes to set the paint. Ask an adult to help.

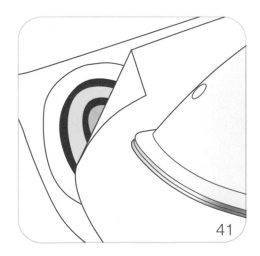

41

5 Pin the right side of each cushion design to the right side of the backing fabric.

Use the dark pink fabric for the lips, orange fabric for the butterfly, and pink fabric for the rainbow.

Now trim the backing pieces.

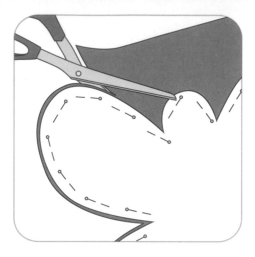

6 Stitch each cushion following the edge of the black painted outline. Leave a 4-inch (10.2-cm) opening on each cushion for stuffing!

7 Make small notches with the scissors in the corners and curves of each cushion.

This will make it easier when you turn the cushions to the right side.

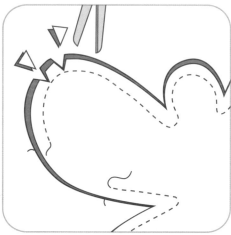

8 Turn the cushions right side out and push out all the corners and edges.

Iron each cushion again with a cloth on top.

9 Use small handfuls of polyester filling to stuff each cushion.

Make sure you stuff the filling into the corners first.

Be patient when stuffing and you will have a better result!

10 Neatly hand-stitch the openings on each cushion.

Some really cool cushions to funk up your room!

butterfly pattern

lips pattern

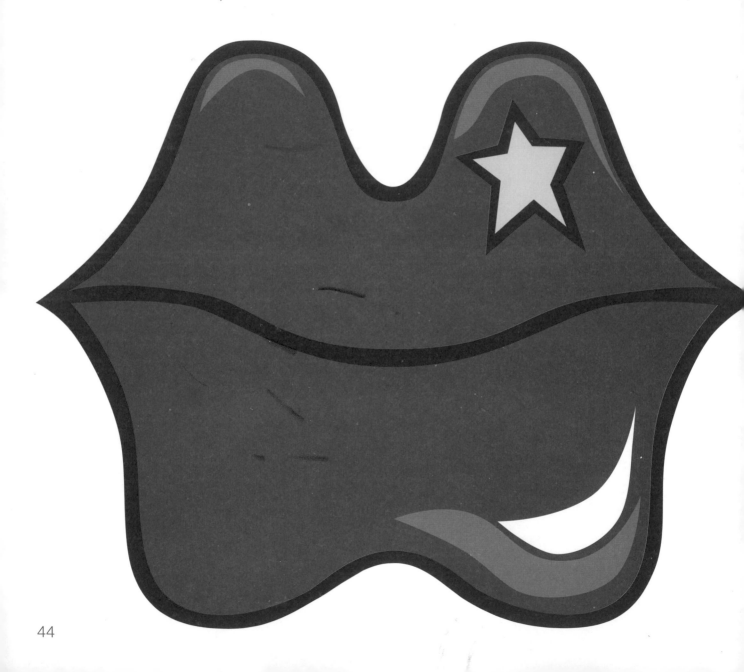

rainbow pattern

tissue box

46

things you need

- empty tissue box
- poster board
- ruler
- pencil & eraser
- blue cotton fabric
- spray adhesive & craft glue
- tracing paper
- scissors & craft knife
- felt — white, pink, orange, yellow, green & purple

1 Cut off the bottom section of the tissue box and cut down the four sides with a craft knife.

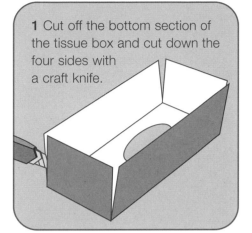

2 Lay the flattened box on the poster board. Trace the outside edge and the tissue opening in the middle.

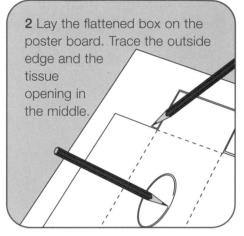

3 Remove the original box and draw a new line 1/4 inch (6 mm) outside your traced line, but don't extend the tissue opening. Next add 1/2 inch (1.3 cm) extra onto the four sides.

4 Now you can erase your original tracing line, except for the tissue opening. Cut around the new outside pencil lines and tissue opening with a craft knife.

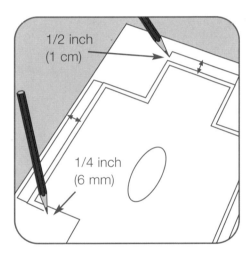

1/2 inch (1 cm)

1/4 inch (6 mm)

5 Attach the poster board piece to the wrong side of the fabric using the spray adhesive. Cut out the fabric, allowing 1 inch (2.5 cm) extra around the edge of the poster board.

Pierce the fabric in the center of the tissue opening with the point of the scissors and cut the fabric around the opening into small strips.

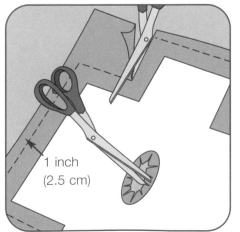

1 inch (2.5 cm)

6 Apply craft glue to the poster board around the tissue opening, then fold back the fabric and glue it to the poster board. Trim the fabric to make it neat.

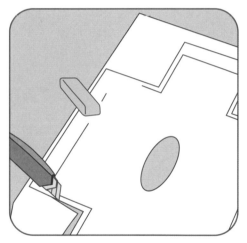

47

7 Score the four lines joining the corners of the poster board, using the point of the scissors and a ruler, and bend the four scored lines in to form the box shape.

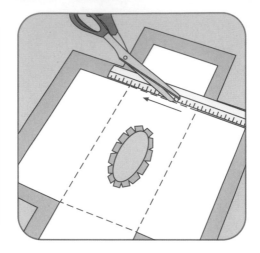

8 Fold the fabric on the two ends over onto the poster board.

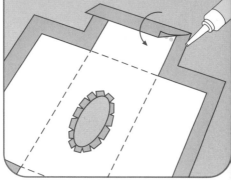

9 Fold the two end pieces of poster board over, and glue down the fabric at the ends of the side pieces. Don't glue the poster board down, just the fabric!

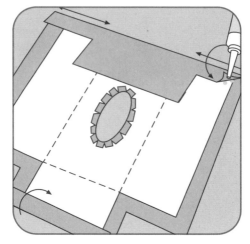

10 Apply craft glue to the L-shaped fabric in the corners of one side of the box and, when the glue is tacky, join the corners together and hold till dry.

Do the same on the other side.

Fold in the remaining two pieces of fabric over inside the box and glue them down.

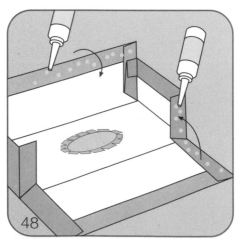

11 Transfer the rainbow, stars (one of each color), one large cloud, and two small clouds onto poster board and cut out.

Glue the matching color of felt onto each side of each star and trim the edges. Cover both sides of the clouds with white felt.

12 Glue the rainbow onto pink felt (both sides) and trim. Use the pattern to cut pieces of orange, green, and purple felt to decorate one side of the rainbow.

Glue all the pieces onto the tissue box just like in the photograph.

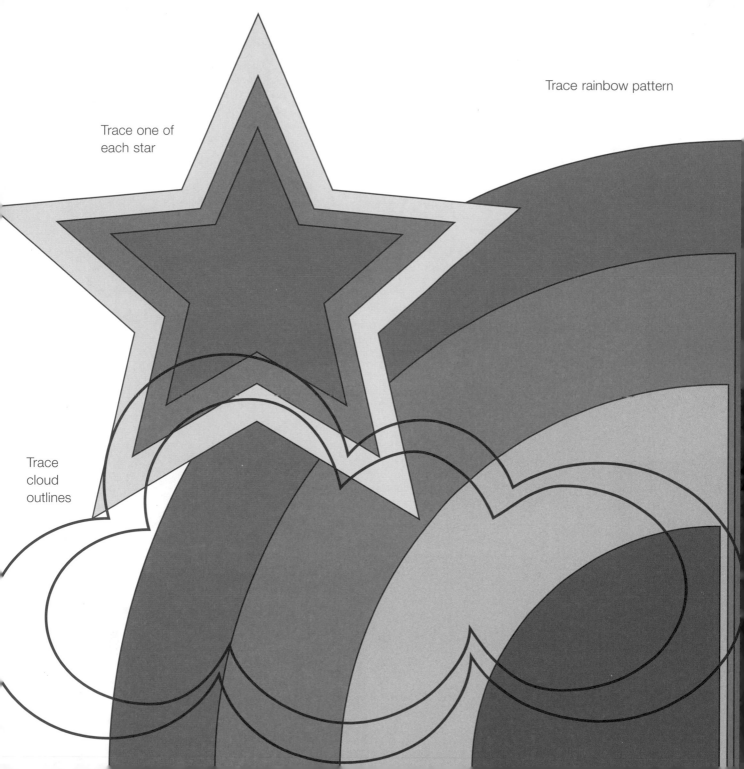

Trace one of each star

Trace rainbow pattern

Trace cloud outlines

painted
flowers

step it
up!

50

things you need

- large sheet of foam board
- acrylic paints —pink, red, blue, green, orange, purple, white & black
- medium paintbrush
- pencil
- craft knife
- craft glue
- double-sided tape

1 Transfer the pattern pieces (pages 52 & 53) for each vase of flowers onto the foam board. You can make the flowers and vases as big as you like!

Cut out the shapes, allowing an extra 1/2 inch (1.3 cm) outside of the pencil lines.

2 Paint the black outlines first, let dry, and then paint the flowers and vases. Use the white paint to lighten the colored paint. Use darker paint for the shading.

3 Glue the flowers and leaves onto the stems and then glue the stems to the back of the vases.

Attach your groovy flowers to the wall with double-sided tape.

A really cool idea is to glue a small box onto the back of the vase. weigh it down with pebbles, and stand it on a table!

things you need

- lampshade
- felt—green, pink, purple & orange
- 4 star gemstones
- small feather boa—purple
- craft glue
- tape measure
- pins
- scissors
- pencil & paper

1 Wrap the piece of green felt around the shade and mark with pins around the top and bottom edges of the shade, and where the felt pieces overlap.

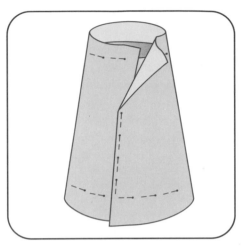

2 Remove the felt and cut out, allowing 2 inches (5 cm) extra on the top and bottom edges and where it overlaps.

Check that the felt piece fits around the shade.

Your piece of felt should look like this!

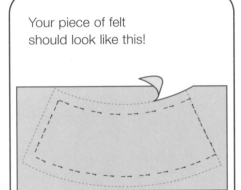

3 Working on small sections at a time, apply craft glue to the shade. Position the felt around the shade and glue the small sections down.

Smooth out any creases as you go.

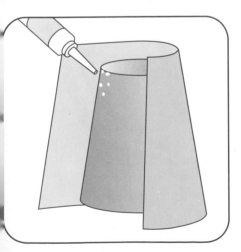

4 Where the ends overlap, glue down one end and cut back the other end until it only overlaps by 1 inch (2.5 cm) and apply glue to the top.

5 Trim the felt on the top and bottom edges so that the felt only just turns over onto the inside of the shade, and glue down.

6 Glue the feather boa around the top and bottom of the shade, overlapping the ends slightly.

Sassy!

7 Trace the star patterns on the next page and cut out four large pink felt hearts, four medium purple hearts, and four small orange hearts.

Glue them together in layers, with a star gemstone in the center. Then glue them onto your shade.

What a hip way to light up your room!

star patterns

storage boxes

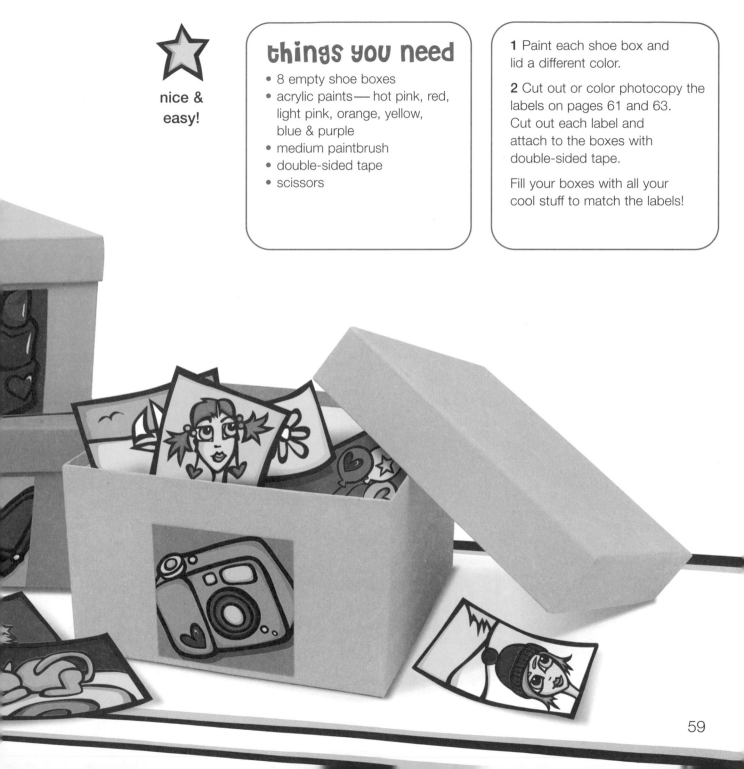

nice & easy!

things you need

- 8 empty shoe boxes
- acrylic paints— hot pink, red, light pink, orange, yellow, blue & purple
- medium paintbrush
- double-sided tape
- scissors

1 Paint each shoe box and lid a different color.

2 Cut out or color photocopy the labels on pages 61 and 63. Cut out each label and attach to the boxes with double-sided tape.

Fill your boxes with all your cool stuff to match the labels!

labels for storage boxes

labels for storage boxes

ISBN 0-439-83406-6

12 11 10 9 8 7 6 5 4 3 2 1   6 7 8 9 10 11/0

Printed in China
First Scholastic printing, February 2006